AMAZING SNAKES!

SPITTING COBRAS

BY EMILY ROSE OACHS

EPIC

BELLWETHER MEDIA • MINNEAPOLIS, MN

EPIC BOOKS are no ordinary books. They burst with intense action, high-speed heroics, and shadows of the unknown. Are you ready for an Epic adventure?

This edition first published in 2014 by Bellwether Media, Inc.

No part of this publication may be reproduced in whole or in part without written permission of the publisher. For information regarding permission, write to Bellwether Media, Inc., Attention: Permissions Department, 5357 Penn Avenue South, Minneapolis, MN 55419.

Library of Congress Cataloging-in-Publication Data

Oachs, Emily Rose, author.
  Spitting Cobras / by Emily Rose Oachs.
      pages cm. – (Epic. Amazing Snakes!)
  Summary: "Engaging images accompany information about spitting cobras. The combination of high-interest subject matter and light text is intended for students in grades 2 through 7."– Provided by publisher.
  Audience: Ages 7-12.
  Includes bibliographical references and index.
  ISBN 978-1-62617-095-7 (hardcover : alk. paper)
  1. Spitting cobras–Juvenile literature. I. Title.
  QL666.O64O33 2014
  597.96'42–dc23
                        2013037803

Printed in the United States of America, North Mankato, MN.

TABLE OF CONTENTS

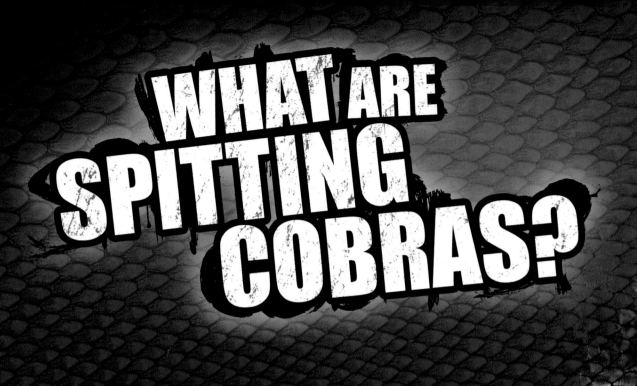

WHAT ARE SPITTING COBRAS?

Spitting cobras are dangerous **venomous** snakes. There are many different kinds. The longest ones can be almost 9 feet (2.7 meters) long!

Spitting cobras come in many different colors. They can have red, black, brown, yellow, or gray **scales**. Some spitting cobras have striped skin.

Colorful Names

Many spitting cobras earn their name from the color of their scales. These include red spitting cobras and zebra spitting cobras.

WHERE SPITTING COBRAS LIVE

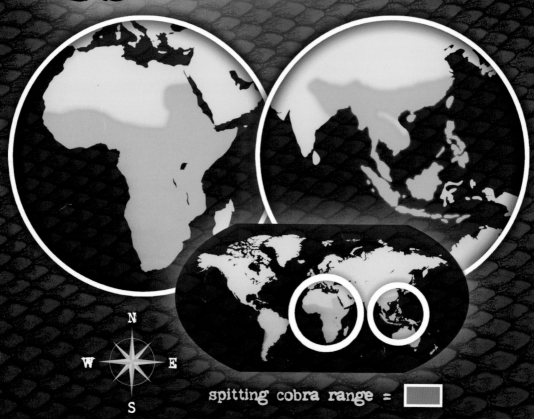

spitting cobra range = ▮

The cobras are found in Africa and southeastern Asia. Some spitting cobras live in dry savannahs

PREY AND PREDATORS

Spitting cobras usually hunt at night. They search for eggs, toads, and birds to eat. They use their **fangs** to **inject** deadly **venom** into **prey**. Then they swallow animals whole!

Spitting Cobra Prey

Mongooses often hunt spitting cobras. They attack before the cobras can defend themselves. Monitor lizards also make spitting cobras into meals.

DEFENSE

Spitting cobras flatten their necks when frightened. First they lift their head. Then they form a **hood** with the skin around their neck. This makes them look larger to scare **predators**.

Back Off!
Spitting cobras also hiss to frighten their predators.

Spitting cobras also spray venom at their enemies. Their fangs have tiny holes in front. They squeeze neck muscles to squirt venom out of the holes.

Spitting Distance
The spray can reach up to 8 feet (2.4 meters)!

Spitting cobras aim for the eyes of their attackers. The venom stings their eyes. Sometimes it causes blindness. Meanwhile, spitting cobras slither to safety.

Not So Bad?

The venom is harmless if it lands on skin.

SPECIES PROFILE

SCIENTIFIC NAMES:	*AFRONAJA* SUBGENUS, MOST OF *NAJA* SUBGENUS; *HEMACHATUS HAEMACHATUS*
AVERAGE SIZE:	2.1 FEET-8.9 FEET (0.65 METERS-2.7 METERS)
HABITATS:	FORESTS, GRASSLANDS, SAVANNAHS
RANGE:	SUB-SAHARAN AFRICA, EGYPT, SOUTHEASTERN ASIA
VENOMOUS:	YES
HUNTING METHOD:	VENOMOUS BITE
COMMON PREY:	LIZARDS, TOADS, BIRDS, EGGS

GLOSSARY

fangs—sharp, hollow teeth; venom flows through fangs and into a bite.

hood—the skin that spreads around a cobra's head and neck; cobras use hoods to scare their attackers.

inject—to force a liquid into something; venomous snakes inject venom into the bodies of prey.

predators—animals that hunt other animals for food

prey—animals that are hunted by other animals for food

savannahs—grasslands with scattered trees

scales—small plates of skin that cover and protect a snake's body

venom—a poison created by a snake; snakes use this venom to hurt or kill other animals.

venomous—able to create venom in their bodies; spitting cobras release venom through their fangs.

TO LEARN MORE

At the Library

Roza, Greg. *Poison! The Spitting Cobra and Other Venomous Animals*. New York, N.Y.: PowerKids Press, 2011.

Sexton, Colleen. *Cobras*. Minneapolis, Minn.: Bellwether Media, 2010.

Willebrandt, Avery. *Spitting Cobra*. New York, N.Y.: Gareth Stevens, 2012.

On the Web

Learning more about spitting cobras is as easy as 1, 2, 3.

1. Go to www.factsurfer.com.

2. Enter "spitting cobras" into the search box.

3. Click the "Surf" button and you will see a list of related Web sites.

With factsurfer.com, finding more information is just a click away.

INDEX

The images in this book are reproduced through the courtesy of: Biosphoto/ SuperStock, front cover, pp. 9, 20; Visuals Unlimited, Inc./ Joe McDonald/ Getty Images, p. 5; Biosphoto/ Daniel Heuclin, pp. 6-7; Juniors Bildarchiv/ Glow Images, p. 10; Boonchuay Promjiam, p. 11 (top, middle); PhotonCatcher, p. 11 (bottom); Maria Gaellman, p. 12; Andre Coetzer, p. 13; Vaughan Jessnitz, p. 15; CB2/ ZOB/ Newscom, pp. 11, 16; Stu Porter, pp. 16-17; Myimagine, p. 18; Exactostock/ SuperStock, p. 19.